The Mind Of Christ In You

The Mind Of Christ In You

by

Jonah Awodeyi

Edited by firstediting.com

Sponsored by New Life Teaching Ministries

ISBN – 978-1-4461-9354-9

Published by Lulu.com

Acknowledgement

I thank God for the privilege of writing this book for all to read and response to "His goodwill towards all mankind". Like many other Christian books, lot of prayers, spiritual thoughts and discussions had taken place in order to be well represented.

The book does not make any claim to have sap the wisdom and depth of the topic discussed. But I pray and trust God to richly bless all that read it more than I was blessed in writing its contents.

Thanks to my Christian friends, especially Dr kayode Okeowo, for their encouragement and support. May I also thank Rev. Amos Komolafe for his contribution and spiritual guidance. Thanks to Rev Grace Komolafe, my sister, who has supported me spiritually, mentally, and financially during this time writing.

Lastly I thank God for my wife, Lydia, and children Elizabeth, Dorcas, and Enoch for their constant support. May God bless you all abundantly.

Contents

Introduction

The message of this book is simple but serious; for it presents the perfect plan of God to restore His precious creation – Man – back to his origin. At man's creation, he possesses a perfect mind, and was capable to think like the Almighty. But he lost this perfection when he disobeyed divine instruction, to possess a perverse mind.

There is no distinction between mankind, Jews or Gentile; all possess a wicked mind. To the Jews it is written, "Their minds were hardened; for until this day at the reading of the old covenant the same veil remains un-lifted" 2 Corinthians 3:14. And to the Gentile, the rest of mankind, it is written "the god of this world has blinded the minds of the unbelieving" 2 Corinthians 4:3. Likewise we read that "Christ is the wisdom of God", emphasising God's providence in Christ Jesus for all mankind in His endeavour to restore mankind to his original state.

Therefore it is said of all who accept the new proposition that they "have the mind of Christ". Man's constant attempt to resolve his situation and reinstate his lost of a perfect mind by creed, thinking, psychoanalysis, or spirituality, failed. Without the mind of Christ, mankind is still far away from his Creator: for it is written, "your thoughts are not my thoughts".

In order to focus our attention on this message and the blessing it contains I have considered the mind of Christ in man from its source through to its restoration.

In addition I have also drawn parallelisms between the life of Jesus during His earthly ministries and that of mankind. This will enable us to see clearly what man should have been without his wicked mind compared to what he is today.

This is evidence in our world as everyone (governments, groups, or individual) does what is right in his or her own eyes, because there is no sound direction. Police reports from each country show the rise in every form of criminology – from lying and deception to violence and terrorism. Man everywhere live in fear. Jesus knew this would be the case when He predicted that "people's heart will faint for fear" towards the end of the world.

Divine intervention is needed, and this commences with the restoration of man's mind to that of Christ's. Hence the message is for all mankind to read regardless of religious statues.

Chapter One

The Source of Christ's Mind in You

"We have the mind of Christ" 1 Corinthians 2:16

*I*t was the Sunday morning before my wife, Lydia, travelled to visit her mother, who is in her 80s. She had just finished praying and suddenly broke the silence by saying, 'Isn't it amazing how God created our minds?' I quietly waited for the follow up to that sudden revelation. Of course I received it when she continued. 'He made our minds able to conceive all these evil thoughts so that we may have them renewed in order to focus on Him,' she concluded.

If this comment was meant to invoke a deep spiritual discussion, I was not going to let it pass by. In order to demonstrate my spiritual depth, I contributed by saying, 'But God did not make this mind.' 'Of course I know God did not make this mind; you know what I meant,' she responded. She read me like a book and was aware that I was trying to show off my spiritual knowledge.

It is true that God did not make this mind. In the beginning when God made man according to scripture, He created him with a perfect mind since he was made in the perfect likeness of his maker according to Gen 1:26 – "then God said 'let us make man in our image, according to our likeness'".

The fundamental truth behind this passage and its depth of revelation may never be completely grasped until we all stand face to face before our maker, and compare the likeness. It is impossible to comprehend the gravity of creation in our present state of mind because the glory of God departed man at the fall of man in the garden. Many spiritual men of God, from generation to generation, have only managed to reveal to us in parts according to their understanding. According to Paul "we know in part, and prophesies in part, but when the perfect comes the partial will be done away; now I know in part, but then I shall know fully just as I also have been known" (1 Corinthians 13: 8-12).

The depth of creating mankind may never be fully understood on this side of eternity until we encounter our maker face-to-face. Nevertheless, we are compelled to pen down whatever partial revelation the Holy Spirit may grant us for the edification of one another.

Genesis 1:26 tells us that man was created in the likeness of his creator, however, a better way to understand this creative business in the image and likeness of God is to turn our attention to Hebrews 1:3 where Jesus was presented as the impressed image of God. It reads "who being the brightness of His glory, and the express image of His person". This same comment is found in Colossians 1:15, 2:9 where it states that all the fullness of deity dwells within Jesus in bodily form.

Adam, on the other hand, had a deity form when the breath of the living God was imparted into his being, thereby making him a possessor of the divine life ("Then the LORD GOD formed man of dust from the ground, and breathed into his nostrils the breath of life; and man became a living being" Genesis 2:7). Without this it was impossible for Adam to exist as a person. Perhaps he existed as a clayed image of the divine, but not as a living being like the divine.

In the King James translation of this passage, man became a living Soul. The Hebrew word translated 'being or soul' is 'naphash', which means 'a breathing creature, or a living organism, or the invisible spiritual part of man'. The root of the word has several usages in the scripture. Sometimes it's used to mean 'breath', – the vital spirit or the principle of life that departs at death from the body, or used to denote mind and rationality (Psalm 57:1), or as the seat of affections, feelings, and emotions (Psalm 35:9).

Whatever usage is embarked upon, it is clear that the soul of man is a separate entity from man's body, and it leaves the body of clay at the point of death to return to its Creator (Originator). According to Colossians 3:10, the personality of Adam was the true knowledge of the image of the One who created him, just as the Christians (believers) "have put on the new self who is being renewed to a true knowledge according to the image of the One who created him". As a result, it is written in Acts 17:28 "for in Him we live and move and exist' and that 'we are His offspring". Consequently, since Adam was His offspring, his divine nature was unquestionable.

From these passages we begin to understand the creation passages in relation to Jesus Christ because both posses the image of the living God in existence. Though our imagination may fall short of the reality of both divine natures, we have a notable record of those who lived, walked, talked, and ate with Jesus, essentially affirming Jesus' life style. It is also possible to grasp this understanding through the Holy Spirit that our first father, Adam, was like Jesus. He was in the complete form of a deity and the brightness of God's glory, exercising a perfect mind. Hence the scripture says 'we have the mind of Christ' which was imparted into Adam at creation, and into believers at the new creation, through rebirth in the Holy Spirit according to John 3:3-6 ("unless one is born of water and the Spirit, he cannot enter into the kingdom of God").

The efficiency and perfection of this mind was immediately put into test at creation when God, in His mercies and graciousness, gave man authority and dominion over all He had created ("and God blessed them; and God said to them 'Be fruitful and multiply, and fill the earth, and subdue it; and rule over the fish of the sea and over the birds of the sky, and over every living thing that moves on the earth" Genesis 1:28). This was an act of trust and confidence in man to be able to execute perfect and godly judgement over the rest of creation as He builds a relationship with him.

In addition, God also entrusted Adam to name every living thing He created, including 'woman'. God never disputed with Adam regarding his choice. Every name was deemed the best choice, just as God Himself would have pronounced. Genesis 2:19 reads "and whatever the man called the living creatures that was its name" shows a complete designation of power and authority. Even the naming of the woman (literally meaning 'she-man, or womb-man or man with a womb, or female-man in the Hebrew words root) was pleasing to God. Amazingly, Adam predicted the woman's role in their relationship as the mother of their offspring, though God called her a playmate or partner.

All these were possible because he had the mind of Christ who created all things. There may have been other things that Adam did during this state of mind - the mind of Christ – that were not recorded in scripture, but shall be revealed when we all assemble in paradise. But we know that he was able to communicate with God at the highest level, if not God's level. He had a perfect relationship and fellowship with God, just as Jesus had. God may have referred to him as His son, boasting of his perfection in the presence of the Angels. In fact, Luke was bold to call him the Son of God in his genealogy account ("the son of Enosh, the son of Seth, the son of Adam, the son of God" Luke 3:38).

We do not know the duration of this relationship before Adam's disobedience, but we know from Genesis that things began to decline when the relationship was temporarily halted until a solution was found. The folly of man's life without fellowship or relationship with God, his creator, began to unfold as man drifted into emptiness. What made man perfect was completely gone. The mind of Christ that was to lead him into all truth and godliness was gone. The bible clearly indicates that Adam was not deceived by the deceiver (Satan), who was offering him what he already had – the godly nature. 1 Timothy 2:14 states "it was not Adam who was deceived, but the woman being quite deceived fell into transgression".

The mind wonders what would have been the outcome if Adam had not disobeyed the godly instructions. Unfortunately he did, and his children inherited emptiness. The great Apostolic Father's conclusion was that 'man's soul is restless until he finds its peace in God'. This sums up the story of our loss in Adam. Though it was over for Adam, it was not over for God. In fact, it activated God's mercies to rescue the situation. Hence, the writer of Hebrews declares 'there is a rest for the people of God' and that all mankind must strive to enter this rest (Hebrews 4). Our desire must be panting for God our Creator so that He, in His mercies, should restore us into His fellowship. Anything other than this falls short of the mind of Christ and a hunger for perfection.

May God grant this request to us in this life and the life to come. Amen.

Chapter Two

Perversion of Christ's Mind in You

*"And God saw that the wickedness of man was great in the
earth and that every intent of the thoughts of his hearts (mind,
soul, spirit) was only evil continually. And the Lord was
sorry that He had made man on earth, and He was grieved in
His heart" Genesis 6:5,6.*

What went wrong? Why has man's perfect mind of
Christ reached such a low that it caused God to repent
and feel sorry for creating man on earth? Man's situation
and his state of mind quickly deteriorated from beauty to
ashes - from supreme perfection to the dustbin of evil -
and it breaks God's heart. The present day out-burst
from God would be 'Oh No, what have I done? I have
created a monster instead of a deity, a pauper instead of
a prince. Adam has lost his mind. It is difficult to
describe what he has turned into. A perfect son turned
sinner; and a friend turned an adversary'.

Reading the words in this passage (Genesis 6:5,6)
brings tears to my eyes, and I suppose will bring tears to
the eyes of anyone who understood the gravity of what
we lost in Adam. Man has not only managed to destroy
its mind but has successfully broken God's heart and

caused him to grieve. We may never know or understand the eternal magnitude of this verse until we enter into eternity with God. Humanly speaking, we can only attribute these verses as spell of surprises and shock, or as an internal feeling of disappointment, regrets, and sorrow on God's side. It is painful to realise that these agony came to being as a result of one act of disobedience.

Please note that God's curse or punishment was not imposed on Adam's mind, but on his desire for food since he will now have to fend for himself. "In toil you shall eat of it (ground) all the days of your life" Gen.3:17. Therefore nothing in the punishment referred to the reason for man's corrupted mind as indicated in Genesis 6. Instead God proceeded to plan on how He will destroy the friendship, which the woman (Eve) struck with the Serpent (Satan). Besides, God provided clothing for Adam to demonstrate His love for His son. However, the question on when did Adam lose his perfect mind still remains a puzzle; the mind that gave names to every living creature including the woman; and the mind that was to rule the earth in the perfect knowledge of His creator.

I submit that man lost his perfect mind when he ate the forbidden fruit. The perfect mind, which is the mind of Christ, was immediately converted to a rational mind since the eating of the fruit is from logic. Thus, Adam instantly possessed a reasoning mind, which was what the serpent (Satan) offered him. Adam was never going to be like God, but have a mind that doubt God's words.

This is evidenced in Adam's reaction to his nakedness as he resulted to the use of leaves, regardless of the size, to cover his nudeness. He must have known from experience that the leaves would dry up at some point, thereby unable to provide him with a lasting cover. Is that the best this wise man could provide for his wife and himself? This is appalling. If only he had retained his mind he would have been able to think like God and provide leather jackets and leather pants for both of them. Instead his mind was focused on leaves. What a future disaster; and what a merciful and friendly God to foresee the future and prevent it from occurring.

I bet the repercussions of his choice later dawned on him when he compared his to that of God. Can you imagine the awkwardness if God had not intervened when He did? Mankind would be wrapped in leaves all day long and every day, for his or her lifetime. I suppose the nudes of today's society would have applauded Adam's choice. On the contrary, God would not permit it because of His everlasting love.

Before we go any further, let us consider the fruit that Adam ate for a moment. Earlier, I said Adam received the instructions, not Eve; hence the sin was Adam's alone. I shall explain this in more detail later. We know that God created this special tree (of course not an apple tree as some may have us believe) in the garden for a purpose, hence the special instruction not to eat from the tree. The tree, according to Genesis 2:16,17 is called 'the tree of the knowledge of good and evil'. We could say that this is the name of the tree just as we have another tree named the tree of life (Gen 3:22); or we could assume that the tree bears two kinds of fruits, namely 'good and evil'. But this second position is not supported in scriptures, nor did Jesus, who taught that a tree couldn't bear two kinds of fruit ("for there is no good tree which produces bad fruit: nor, on the other hand, a bad tree which produce good fruit" Luke 6: 43-45) embrace it.

Besides, we also know by nature that this is impossible. So we can easily eliminate this thought from our imagination and retain the first that assumed the name of the tree to be 'good and evil'. One thing is certain, we know that Adam was created in God's likeness (image); therefore, without sin just as Jesus, the second Adam, was born into the world sinless. We also know that God was very pleased with His creation that He declared it to be 'good'. So was Adam, who was created in the image of the all-good God. Therefore, in order for this tree to produce the knowledge of good and evil, the fruit of the tree must be evil.

Bearing in mind that nothing evil was in Adam at creation, we now could perceive how the eating of the tree's fruit could contaminate Adam's personality. The evil fruit permeates Adam's natural being to create dual personalities, which Adam will not be able to control. God knew the tree was nothing but grief and evil, hence the warning not to partake of its fruit. He knew that eating it would destroy Adam and his generations to come, as evident in Genesis 6, since it is a deadly poison. Moreover, God was very helpful to Adam by giving him the precise location of the tree – the centre of the garden – so that he may not accidentally eat the fruit. The tree was, in fact, distinctly isolated from the rest of the edible things (trees or fruits). Although it is an evil tree its purpose in creation was good; hence the testing for obedience.

We tend to believe that Adam and Eve lived with this tree for a considerable period before Eve decided to focus her attention on the tree. She must have constantly asked Adam why such a beautiful fruit remained uneatable and forbidden by God. One day she found someone who was ready to provide an interesting answer.

I pointed the finger at Adam as the offender, and not Eve, because she was not created at the time of the instruction given to Adam. She may have received the instruction from Adam who was readily prepared to obey God without any question. This may explain her curiosity to find an answer. Besides, God made His intentions clear after the act of defiance by first questioning Adam before Eve. However, this does not excuse her act of disobedience to God even if the instructions were from Adam.

On the other hand, it is extremely difficult to explain Adam's reason for eating the fruit, for according to scriptures he was not deceived (1 Timothy 2:14). He willingly listened to the voice of the woman and readily partook of the forbidden fruit. Noticeably, the fruit was not given by the Serpent but rather by Eve who experienced no change after eating the forbidden fruit.

Some may call it an act of love for his wife, while others may see it as an answer to the embedded questions in his mind. Some others may see it as an opportunity to be like God. But why does he want to be someone he already was since he was created in the image of God? Why was he not satisfied with being good that he eagerly wanted to be evil and complicate things? I suppose only Adam knows why he momentarily decided to respond to his wife's intuition or newly acquired revelation.

Sadly, the effect of the poison (evil) was manifested immediately as the accusation and pointing of fingers mounts up. Adam accused his wife who accused the serpent. The bond of love and fellowship was quickly broken since both now possess dual personalities and fault finding. The 'past the blame parcel' was born as no one was ready to be responsible for the unfortunate situation. While Adam blamed God for giving him the woman, the woman blamed the serpent for deceiving her. Adam said to God "the woman whom thou gave to be with me; she gave me from the tree, and I ate" (Genesis 3:12). In today's language we will say 'it's not my fault; it's Yours (God). I would not have eaten the fruit if the woman you gave me had not passed it on to me. You know I did not eat the fruit when I was alone in the garden, and may not have eaten it had you not given me this woman. Therefore, it is your fault I ate it'. God knew this would be the outcome for eating the fruit, hence the strict warning "The day that you eat from it you shall surely die" Genesis 2:17.

Trust in the goodness of God and good will among men is thrown out of the window as fellowship with one another is destroyed. The good intention of God backfired as division reigned supreme. The mind of Christ in Adam was contaminated and corrupted as he paid the cost to becoming god. But we read about the second Adam, Jesus, in Philippians 2:6, in the following statements: "Who, although He existed in the form of God, did not regard equality with God a thing to be grasped". But this was not the case with Adam who thought that equality with God was a thing to be grasped. So when his wife presented the opportunity to him on a platter, he did not hesitate to grasp it.

Every one of us still possesses this evil mind to become or play god; but never prepared to bear the responsibilities for our actions. When I became a Christian, my pastor told us a story (parable) about a blind man who was a beggar because of his situation. Every day he walked up and down the busy street singing a persuasive and sympathetic song that blames Adam for his blindness. 'My blindness was as a result of Adam's sin' he sang. 'If Adam had not sinned I won't have lost my sight. If Adam had not sinned I won't have been poor and begging for money, life would have been a better place for me to live'. As passer-bys heard this song they drop some pennies into his begging bowl.

One blessed day a wealthy man heard this beggar's song and was sympathetic with him. So he stopped, invited the beggar to his palace, healed his blindness, and gave him free accommodation to live. This was not just a bed and breakfast; it was abundant eating to the satisfaction of the beggar. It was a first class royal treatment. But there was a condition, which the beggar must observe during his stay at this rich man's palace. There is a room in the palace reserved for the rich man, which no one must enter. This ruling also applies to the beggar. Opening the door of this room was punishable by dismissal from the palace. The beggar agreed to abide by this rule.

As time went by the beggar, in his comfort, began to ponder and inquire why the room was a forbidden ground and what could have been hidden inside that would be so important to the rich man. Since no one had the answer to his troubled mind, he decided to open the door and have a peep while no one was around. Besides, his intentions were never to enter the room, as careful as possible, and hoped the master of the house wouldn't mind or notice when he comes home. Perhaps the room contains the best things reserved by the master for personal use, he pondered daily.

So one day he opened the door of the room and found that it was empty. There wasn't any decoration, nor do ornaments inside except for a worn-out shoe, torn rags and a begging bowl (the beggar's old belongings). So he was disappointed and shut the door.

But when the master arrived that evening he noticed that the door had been opened because there was dust on the hall carpet. He made an enquiry to find out who had disobeyed his order. When he found out that it was the beggar, he instructed his servants to send him away in his begging rags, shoes, and bowl, saying to him 'you must never blame Adam for your misfortune ever again, for you had all the comfort in the world, but you were unable to abide by a simple rule'. The beggar was thrown out to the street from where he came with no excuse to sing about.

This somehow typified the punishment imposed on Adam when God reminded him that he was made from dust, and to the dust he shall return. To this present day, and until the return of Christ Jesus, mankind is lumbered with dual personality and you never know which of his personality will show up. According to Romans 1:21f, mankind has lost its divine given mind to a perverse mind; for we read "even though they knew God, they did not honour Him as God, or give thanks, but they became futile in their speculation and their foolish heart was darkened. Professing to be wise they became fools". So God gave mankind up and over to evil spirits – Sexual impurity, Shameful lusts, and Depraved mind. To be more specific, the definitions of these terms are as follows -

Sexual impurity – the worship of sexually permissive gods and goddesses (falling angels known as demons just as it was in the days of Noah in Genesis 6)

Shameful lusts are all sexual acts outside the bond of marriage, lesbianism, homosexuality, and all kinds of animalistic sexual acts, including sexual acts with animals, babies/children and pornography.

Depraved mind – is the mind that is filled with every kind of wickedness, evil, greed, and depravity. The

27

mind has being perverted and all that is in it is nothing but continuous evil because mankind still chooses to listen to the voice for power, authority, and greediness rather than the voice of God.

You may think you could have done better than Adam and the beggar given the opportunities they both had, but I doubt if your curiosity for more power, to grasp equality with God, would not have prevailed. For wherever there is a forbidden ground the mind ponders for the unknown and waits for the opportune time to enquire. It is generally said that 'curiosity kills the cat'; thus, man's mind is always pondering the unknown, especially that which has been declared harmful, to his doom. Our depraved mind teaches us nothing else but to grasp power for self, regardless of the outcome or who is hurt on our way to power, and greediness.

We assert and teach our children that we are created in the image of an animal, and we behave exactly like one because we possess an animalistic mind from Adam. Accordingly, 2 Peter 2:12 sates that we are "like brute beasts, creatures of instinct, born only to be caught and destroyed, and like beasts we too shall perish". Some sell themselves for money and power; while some backstab, manipulate, and cheat their way to power. Little or no consideration is given to the weak and helpless. The reward is abuse, pain, and stressful life. We behave just like Absalom in 2 kings 15-18, who plotted to oust his father, David, by using his charm and good looks to persuade the community.

Our society teaches us to be brutal, selfish, and to have an ego; and that only those who are weak show mercy. But such teachings are foreign to God who teaches us to be gentle, kind, merciful, and love our neighbours. Jesus said "just as you want people to treat you, treat them in same way" Luke 6:31. Such godly teachings are the mind of Christ. And there is still hope for mankind to change his animalistic behaviour to a godly behaviour through Jesus Christ. This was why Jesus came into the world, as well as why He died a shameful death on the cross, so that He may remove the Adamic shame we inherited in Genesis 3:10.

Chapter Three

The Mind of Jesus in the Gospel

"I have come to do Thy will" Hebrews 10:7

*T*his simple confession by Jesus in Hebrews 10:7 sums up His essential visit to the world. It underlines the basic principle of spiritual commitment and also emphasizes the ground for continuous fellowship with God. Unfortunately, this was the downfall of Adam - the inability to continuously remind himself the main purpose of his existence, which is both the fellowship and worship of God. Once this purpose is defeated, one's goal in life is grounded or at worst is defeated.

Doing the will of God on this side of eternity, prepares us for the real thing when we spend eternity with God and enjoy His fellowship. The psalmist states "in His presence is the fullness of joy and at His right hand is pleasure forever" (Psalm 16:11). It is very challenging to read about the strong determination in Jesus' mind to doing God's will. Nothing was going to stop Him; nor was he going to allow anything to stand in his way or between him and His God. Sometimes we tend to think that doing God's will was so easy for Jesus during His earthly ministry that we forget that the scripture emphasized "He learned obedience to the will of God" as a son (Hebrews 5:8).

At the age of 12 He was found listening and debating the word of God in the temple with educated priests and rulers. The amazing thing was that He was able to communicate with these teachers of the law at their level. Can you imagine the embarrassment of having a 12-year-old boy instructing and correcting these teachers in the presence of hundreds of visiting worshipers? It's like a boy of 12 in a maths or science class instructing the teacher in the presence of the class. Such kids are considered as genius.

His mates have been to the festival, enjoyed their teachings, memorized some verses in scripture, and have had fun with other kids at the festival with the exception of Jesus who continued his debate for three days after the festival. The bible said his parents thought He was with the other kids having fun (Luke 2:43,44). How wrong they were as they finally discovered He was missing. They have left their 12-year-old son behind in Jerusalem. When they eventually found him in the temple He told them that He was in His father's house ("Why is it you are looking for Me? Did you not know that I had to be in My Father's house?" Luke 2:49).

In another incident with the Samaritan woman he said to His disciple "I have food to eat that you do not know about. My food is to do the will of him who sent Me, and complete His work" John 4:32,34. Interestingly, it was food that led to the disobedience and downfall of

Adam. Therefore, it is extremely important that the One God sent to redeem man did not focus on food as its primary purpose. Obedience to the will of God was paramount to the success of His mission on earth as well as among men.

He was equally determined to have God's will proclaimed at His baptism when He declared to John "it is fitting for us to fulfil all righteousness" Matt. 3:15.

Prior to this incident John had acknowledged and proclaimed Him as 'the Lamb of God that takes the sin of the world away'. Though Jesus was unpopular at this time John was the people's man of God, whom Jesus would not undermined. Hence it was important that both show mutual respect, which would glorify God. It was also essential that both parties (Jesus and John the Baptist) fulfilled all righteousness. Any form of disobedience will disqualify any sacrifice rendered.

Therefore, He must first learn and demonstrate obedience to the voice of God before He could be acclaimed and approved as the 'Lamb of God'. Without obedience sacrifice is nothing. Prophet Samuel told King Saul that obedience is better than sacrifice when he stated, "has the Lord as much delight in burnt offerings and sacrifice as in obeying the voice of the Lord? Behold, to obey is better than sacrifice and to heed than the fat of rams" 1 Samuel 15:22. Thus, obedience was crucial and vital to Jesus' entire ministry since it was through the disobedience of the first man, Adam, that sin came into the world.

The act of obedience is also seen in his teaching on praying. He taught His disciples to pray "thy will be done on earth as it is done in heaven" Matthews 6:10. In reference to this verse we know that the angels in heaven are in constant obedience to the will of God. And it is the heart's desire of the Almighty that the people on earth carry out His will; since all act of disobedience will be severely punished. We often overlook this emphasis in the prayer instruction to concentrate on other less important issues, such as the debate if these verses should be recited or be taken as a pattern of praying.

But in my mind, and I suppose in the mind of Jesus, doing God's will on earth was the primary purpose and backbone to having fellowship with God. The sacrifice of Jesus on behalf of man is fruitless without obedience to the will of God. No one would be able to acknowledge the Fatherhood of God without the practising of His will on earth. Neither is the request for daily bread and protection granted in disobedience to His will on earth. Therefore, the disciples must learn that nothing must stand in the path of obedience and total surrender to His will and purpose on earth. This crucial lesson was completely absorbed by the disciples as we read their confession in Acts 4:19. "Whether it is right in the sight of God to give heed to you rather than to God, you be the judge. We must obey God rather than men" they said. Mission accomplished as lesson was taken in and practically applied. Jesus' teaching on obedience to God has prevailed in man's heart and mind;

therefore, nothing else matters. Obedience is the key word to godly living.

In another teaching, this time to the zealot multitude that came to Him to inquire what they can do to do God's work, He simply and firmly emphasized that God's work involves listening to Him in obedience. "This is the work of God, that you believe in Him whom He has sent" (John 6:29), was Jesus' remark.

Every one of us wants to do the work of God, but the first step towards this goal is obedience to the voice of whom He has sent. When Jesus realized his disciples were ready to listen and obey His voice, He commissioned them saying, "as the Father has sent Me I also send you" (John 20:21). Of course he knew they were ready when he heard their confession and total commitment to the lifestyle of obedience. For their confession was "Lord to whom shall we go? You have the words of eternal life; and we have believed and have come to know that you are the Holy one of God" (John 6:68,69). Prior to this confession Jesus granted them the permission to leave, if they so desired (John 6: 66-69).

Doing God's work does not involve performing a miracle, but rather obeying instructions from God. Jesus highlighted this to the Jews by telling them a parable of a father and his two sons. This father asked his second son to go to his farm to work, but the son bluntly refused to go. After a while, and carefully reconsidering his refusal, he changed his mind and went to his father's farm to work. Meanwhile, the father turned his attention to his first son requesting him to go to the farm just like he did with the second son. The first son immediately assured his father that he would definitely obey his instruction, but later failed to carry out his promise. Jesus then went on to ask his audience which of the sons obeyed his father (Matt. 21:28-32). Doubtlessly, we all agreed it was the second son who reconsidered his refusal.

It is also inspiring to notice that the works Jesus did were according to the father's will. In John 5:30 we read, "I can do nothing on my own initiative. As I hear, I judge and my judgement is just because I do not seek my own will but the will of Him who sent me". This does ring a bell as he commissioned his disciples, saying to them "without me you can do nothing" (John 15:5).

The father sent the son, and the son gets initiatives from the father. Now the son sends his disciples and wants them to know that the whole initiative must come from him. Even the Holy Spirit would not speak on His own initiative when He comes, but will convey to the disciples the instructions of Jesus (John 16:13-15).

Therefore, it is important for us to acknowledge the order of service in the Godhead. The Son obeys the Father, the Holy Spirit glorifies both the Son and the Father, and the Father is pleased with the Son that He granted His request to release the Holy Spirit to the disciples. This is beyond any human's understandings. No one truly understands the mind of God except the Holy Spirit. But we now know that the disciples have the mind of Christ through the Holy Spirit, which will eventually lead to the establishment of the will of God on earth.

I never knew that the choosing of disciples was according to the will of God until now. Of course I knew that Jesus prayed all night before selecting his disciples, but I did not realize that God gave Him the names of those to be appointed. According to John 17:6 we read "I manifested Thy name to the men whom Thou gives me out of the world. Thy they were, and Thou gives them to Me, and they have kept Thy word".

So let's set the record straight again. The disciples were the Father's choice and the Son completely accepted His Father's choice. Who were these people chosen by the Father we ask ourselves? Fishermen, a thief, doubters, nationalists, despised tax collector, and a young immature man were the divine's choice. These are the group of people the Father wants the Son to entrust the responsibilities of proclaiming the message of salvation. Wasn't the message important to be conveyed by people of authority and royal standings? What about the learned men of the day, such as the priests, rabbis, and scribes (theological scholars)? Again, were these authorities an powers not good enough for the job at hand, especially when these folks were in great spiritual expectation of the coming messiah?

The scripture clearly says in 1 Corinthians 2:26-29 that God, in His wisdom, has "chosen foolish things of the world to shame the wise, and the weak things of the world to shame the things which are strong, and the base things and the despised of the world, and the things that are not (invisible, common) to nullify the things that are, so that no man should boast before God". Jesus had no choice but to work with this group and transform them to be spiritual giants, through obedience to the Father's will, for the kingdom of God.

What should we say about the choice of Judas, whom Jesus knew God placed there to be the one who will betray Him? From the gospel account we knew Jesus tried so hard to turn things around for Judas. He made him the treasure in order to change his attitude towards money, thereby making him trustworthy. Unfortunately, this failed. He confronted him face-to-face with regards to his betrayer plot, but that was not enough to stop Judas' greed. When all effort failed, He finally told him to quickly carry out his plot. "What you must do, do it quickly" (John 13:27) Jesus said to Judas. Instead of repenting at this point, he paid no attention to Jesus' comment. Nevertheless, Jesus did not stop loving him. Even at the last minute, He called him a friend. According to scripture he 'Immediately went to Jesus and said "Hail, Rabbi" and kisses Him. Jesus said to him "Friend, do what you have come to for"' (Matthew 26:49,50).

Only the Father knew why these different personalities were chosen, and we sincerely thank Him for His choice. The Son was pleased with it; and their performance in the book of Acts of the Apostles manifested they were the best. Without them the Gentiles may not have heard the gospel. We owe them so much, and thank God for their dedication in the face of persecution.

Moreover, the choice of those to be saved was that of the Father. Jesus said "all that the Father gives to Me shall come to me, and the ones who come to me I will not cast out" (John 6:36). In another place He said "Do not grumble among yourselves: no one can come to Me unless the Father who sent Me draws him, and I will raise him up on the last day" (John 6:43,44). Evidently, only those whose names are written in the book of life by the Father get the invitation to come to Jesus. According to verse 45, "everyone who has heard and learnt from the Father" comes to Jesus. The Father decides who comes into His Kingdom.

Since Jesus would not talk or teach about anyone but the Father, He needs someone to talk about Him to the world. The Father's providence is the person of the Holy Spirit, whom Jesus said would teach the disciples all things regarding Him and the Father. To this He said, "but when He, the Spirit of truth, comes, He will guide you into all the truth; for He will not speak on His own initiative, but whatever He hears, He will speak; and He will disclose to you what is to come. He shall glorify Me; for He shall take of Mine, and shall disclose it to you" John 16:13,14. Now is the hour to listen to what the Holy Spirit says about Jesus and the mind of Christ.

In Acts of the Apostles 10:38, the Holy Spirit through Peter states, "you know of Jesus of Nazareth, how God anointed Him with the Holy Spirit and with power; and how he went about doing good, and healing all who were oppressed by the devil, for God was with Him". The key word for us here is 'doing good'. This same knowledge was common to both Jews and Gentiles that

Jesus went about His daily business doing the good that the Holy Spirit reveals.

Mankind has lost this special attribute that was present within him at creation. The ability to be good was far fetched as Jesus clearly acclaimed "there is none good except God" (Matthew 19:17). These days our goodness comes camouflaged with a hidden agenda. It is the overlaying garment of our selfishness and selfish ambitions. When we perform a righteous good deed with selfish motives, we sound our trumpets so loud that the deaf can hear us and applaud. Other time our good deed is conditional.

But Jesus did not act in this manner. His good deeds were unconditional and willing. He did not compel the people to follow him, nor His teaching. Nor was there any expectation of appreciation or 'thank you card' from those He delivered from demonic oppression. Instead, members of this same group added their voices to those of his accusers, to sentence Him to death. His good nature did everything the way the Father willed and it was the Father who did it in and through Him. God's goodness towards mankind never ceases, and is without condition. He initiates Goodness because He is all-good, even to the cross.

Let's look at one more passage before we conclude this section. In 1 Peter 3:2 is a declaration about the mind of Christ as perceived by the disciples. It reads, "who committed no sin nor was any deceit found in His mouth and while being reviled, He did not in return; while suffering he uttered no threats, but kept entrusting

Himself to Him who judges righteously". These words are straightforward and clear for all to see and understand. Jesus kept His cool under pressure and entrusted Himself to God.

Obviously every aspect of Jesus' earthly life was constantly linked to the Father in obedience to doing His will. When the going got tough His eyes remained focused on the Father. Even when His disciples stood their ground to fight the soldiers who came to arrest Him, His words were "the cup which the Father has given Me, shall I not drink it?" (John 18:11). There was no looking back. Though He had the heavenly hosts at His disposal, He refused to ask the Father for an attack on Pilate's army. The agony and pain of the cross did not stop Him from saying a prayer for His persecutors, seeing that He asked the Father not to hold them accountable for their actions against Him. And as He took the last breath His eyes were still focused on the Father, and His last words were "Father into Thy hands I commit my spirit" (Luke 23:46).

From beginning to end of His earthly ministry He demonstrated perfect obedience to God the Father. He knew why He had come into the world, what He was commissioned to do, and the consequences of any acts of disobedience. He could have given up the task as He requested the Father's cup to be taken away from Him three times. But every time, He concluded in His famous slogan "Father not my will but thy will be done" (Luke 22:42).

This is the mind of Christ to be desired by all His disciples; a mind that endlessly repeats and reclaims its stance to do the Father's will in the face of danger, insults, and persecution, declaring "I have come (exist) to do thy will" (Hebrews 10:7). If there was any stubbornness in Jesus' life it was this hardened heart bent on doing God's will on earth, just as the angels do in heaven. Adam failed mankind by choosing not to do God's will on earth but Jesus was very determined to do it though He is the Son of God. It is written about Jesus that "Although He was a Son, He learnt obedience from the things which He suffered" (Hebrews 5:8).

His prayer, teaching, and cry to God and man are simply this: – "THY WILL BE DONE ON EARTH AS IT IS DONE IN HEAVEN". May God in His mercies grant us the mind of Christ that constantly seeks to do His will.

Chapter Four

Restoration of Christ's Mind in You

"I will cleanse you from all your filthiness; and give you a new heart and put a new spirit within you" Ezekiel 36:25,26

*T*he previous chapter revealed to us the complete mess mankind got itself into. As far as God was concerned there is little or no hope for man to redeem himself from his situation. His children have grown wild and gone astray in their thinking, and God regretted He made man. What a disappointment we are. Genesis 6:6 got us in touch with the story as we read "and the Lord was sorry that He made man on the earth, and He was grieved in His heart". The holy and righteous God, who loved us so much, was deeply wounded.

In order to save face, He embarked on destroying the very thing He had created and loved dearly - Man. With the exemption of a family, whom He trusted, He was able to savage something from the mess, while He sent massive flood to destroy everything that lived on earth. Realising He had to rebuild, He preserved marriage and future generations of everything He created in pairs, and revealed to the human family how to escape the flood.

God hoped that this righteous family would redeem the situation and build a righteous community that will enable Him to carry out His proposed plan of sending a redeemer. But it did not take long after the flood to find out that something was definitely wrong with man. His heart has been corrupted. The 'seed of disobedience' has been planted through Adam and was about to sprout again.

As the new family grew and expanded, the seed also sprouted and expanded from family to family in the community. By the time God was aware of this evil plot, as if God was not paying attention, men have taken matters into their hands. This time man's desire and ambition has found its old root to be like God, and live in the heavenly. "Let us build for ourselves a city and a tower whose top will reach into heaven" (Genesis 11:4), was their cry to one another.

This happened about 500 years after the flood of Noah. You would expect the flood story and its evidence to be fresh in the peoples' mind because we know from scripture that Shem, Noah's son, was still alive and must have told the story of the previous wicked generation. Noah also must have encouraged godly living since he died about 150 years before this incident. But there was no way to stop the seed of disobedience from growing and manifesting itself in man's heart. Another judgement was eminent. Another flood was out of the question this time since God must be truthful to His promise to never flood the earth again (Genesis 9:13-17). But God was full of surprises and rich in wisdom. Thus, He invented language barriers by introducing various languages into clans of families, thereby confusing and diffusing man's evil plot (Genesis 11:7-9).

It is obvious God had to do more than flood man's world or create a language barrier in order to remove the deep-seated root of disobedience and the mind full of evil plots. Neither was the choice to create another perfect man and start all over again to achieve His purpose of having a community of people with the mind of Christ on the table. Besides, the original plan and promise was that the seed of the woman should crush the serpent's head. This must be achieved in co-operation with man, or His promise means nothing. He must continue with the original plan and find His way around man's disobedience.

Though people like Abraham, Jacob, Moses, and David played very important roles, living righteously and having deep fellowship with their Creator, they all had flaws in their lives and were unable to bring their family in-line with God's plan and promise. In a nutshell, they all failed to bridge the gap and rescue mankind's misfortunes. The more God tried to weave the cords together the more disappointment He received from man. He deployed the tactic of including women of faith, such as Tamar (Judah's daughter-in-law that played prostitution), Rehab (Canaanite who helps the spies to escape), Ruth (Naomi's daughter-in-law, and a gentile who found faith in the God of Israel), and even

Bathsheba, the wife of murdered Uriah (Mathews 1:2-6), in order to make patches in the plan, which was twisting and turning due to man's flaws. He thereby disregarded the origin, culture and religious difference of the people chosen, in order to accomplish His plan.

Essentially, God had to review the plan by taking matters into His own hands. He must again visit man's world to carry out His plan by Himself. There are three things He must do within a very short time. First, He must come down to show mankind what He expects of them, thereby demonstrating the mind of Christ. Second, He must pay the price for the punishment He dealt to man when Adam knowingly disobeyed His command. The result meant that in man's world evil constantly prevailed and over shadowed good. So, when He was born into the world it did not take man days before human launched the death squad to find and destroy his Creator; thereby demonstrating the evil intents embedded within him (Matthew 2:13-20). Third, He must replace mankind's mind by creating in him a new heart, spirit, and mind, in order to succeed (Ezekiel 11:19,20).

Without this plan, everything else has no footing. It is nice to show mankind how to live a godly life with the mind of Christ, and equally amazing to be punished (die) in their place, but without the change of heart (a new heart, spirit, and mind) the whole plan is a waste of time and effort.

Some people go to prison for the crime they commit, given the opportunity to reflect on their crime. After a while they are pardoned and released back into the society without a change of heart and mind. Later in life they are caught for either the same crime or another and sentenced again. It shows that imprisonment does not eradicate the root of evil in man though the branches were pruned.

God knew this would happen if He failed to incorporate the renewal of heart, spirit and mind into His plan. This, God revealed to His prophet, Ezekiel, many years (about 400 years) before it was implemented. He wrote, "Moreover I will give you a new heart and put a new spirit within you, and I will remove the heart of stone from your flesh (body) and give you a heart of flesh. I will put My Spirit within you and cause you to walk in My statues (commandments), and you will be careful to observe My ordinances (laws)" (Ezekiel 36:26,27). With this heavenly new plan, God solved man's problem both physically and mentally. He eliminated the root of evil in man, and crushed the act of disobedience.

He went the extra mile to ensure that recreating man as in the day of Adam must accomplish His initial promise. Like our proverb rightly says 'you can force the Camel to the water, but cannot make it drink', God knew the 'Camel' must possess a change of heart, the thirst for water, and the willingness to drink.

Consequently, He was going to surgically remove man's stubborn mind and stony heart by uprooting the seed of disobedience that the enemy (Satan) planted long time ago. It was like surgically removing the cancer-affected tissues of the breast, giving it a chemo drug, and blasting it with radiotherapy in order to achieve a complete cure.

God knows it would be fruitless to cut down the tree from its trunk to allow a new branch to grow. So the best option is to uproot the tree and plant a new seed. This was attested by John the Baptist in Matthew 3:10 that "the axe is already laid at the root of the tree" in order to uproot it and plant a new one. Jesus confirmed this plan when He said, "every plant which My heavenly father did not plant shall be rooted up" (Matthew 15:13).

By rooting up every plant that the Father did not plant, a new beginning was declared as well as eminent. Though God was the very Person who planted the first plant, it has become corrupted by evil and unlike what was originally planted. He now sees it as strange plantings, no longer to be pruned because it is corrupted from the root. It must be rooted out. Therefore, God is compelled to give man a new heart and a new spirit that will enable him to defeat Satan this time around.

According to the prophet Jeremiah, God will give man a heart to know Him and focus on Him as it was in the days of Adam in the garden prior to his disobedience "I will give them a heart to know Me, for I am the Lord; and they will be My people, and I will be their God, for they will return to Me with their whole heart" He told the prophet (Jeremiah 24:7). Man will again belong to Him and not to Satan. Therefore, the mind's restoration was essential and must immediately begin, to give mankind a chance of returning to his Maker.

In addition, God is going to plant His Spirit in man to guide and enable him to recognise truth from deceit. According to Jesus, when God's Spirit, the Spirit of truth, is released into man, He will reveal all truth to him ("He will guide you into all the truth" John 16:13). Adam and Eve were fed with lies about God that changed them, their children's lifestyle, as well as their community. Thus, Jesus told the Jews of His days, that they were "the children of their father Satan, for Satan was a murderer from the beginning and does not stand in the truth because there is no truth in him. Whenever he speaks a lie, he speaks from his own nature, for he is a liar and the father of lies" (John 8:44).

God's indwelling Spirit in man makes all the difference to the restoration. His constant presence, guidance, and support seal the deal for God and man. Jesus said "when He, the Spirit of truth comes; He will convince the world concerning Sin, Righteousness and Judgement" (John16:8). Therefore, man will be fully aware of sin, how to live righteously, and will remember that there are repercussions for failing to lead a righteous life. According to Jesus, God had a simple formula: "make the tree good and its fruit will be good" (Matthew 12:33); hence the need to have His Spirit in man to complete the assignment.

So, it is written in 1 John 3:9 "no one who is born of God practices sin, because His seed abides in him" to indicate the presence of God's Spirit in man as a planted seed, thereby affirming God's purpose. It's the planted seed that enables man not to practice sin, and makes the

49

new man-tree a godly tree that produces good fruit. This was God's initial act of creation in Adam before the rebellion that led to his fall. He (the Holy Spirit) is God's catalyst and medication for the poison that the devil planted in man.

After Adam's disobedience and before the flood, God commented "His spirit shall not strive with man forever" (Genesis 6:3). Now, it seems the right action is to reinstate His Spirit in man to enable him to fight Satan and his canny devices, guiding him (man) to make righteous choices, was the best move.

Paul realised this in his letter to the Galatians stating "for in Christ Jesus neither circumcision anything or un-circumcision, but a new creation" (6:15). The one thing that matters to both God and man is the new creation, with its proposed goodness for mankind. "Therefore if any man is in Christ Jesus, he is a new creation, the old things passed away, behold, new things have come to stay" (2 Corinthians 5:17), becomes the pillar and foundation of this gracious plan from the Almighty. It is also written in Ephesians 4:23,24 that the new creation is the new man, which must be "renewed in the spirit of his mind, and put on the new self which, in the likeness of God, has been created in righteousness and holiness of the truth".

The new man is created in the likeness of God, taking us back to the creation story in Genesis; therefore, implying and employing man to re-focus his mind on righteousness, holiness, and truth. This was the fundamental reality of creation and the essential requirement to enter into fellowship with his Creator. The old man believed the lies of the Serpent, but the new man must be firmly rooted in the truth so that worship and fellowship with God could be re-established. "An hour is coming, and now is, Jesus said, when the true worshipers shall worship the Father in Spirit and Truth" (John 4 23).

In this statement, Jesus used His arrival to mark the beginning of this new thing that restores man to fellowship with his Creator. His firm assertion to Nicodemus in John 3, regarding the new birth into the kingdom of God, captures the intentions of the living God. The period for change has arrived and man must be willing to accept it, else he stands no chance of entering into fellowship with his Creator. This does not come about through the union between man and his wife, for the outcome will not be a new beginning, but through the Spirit of God, so that Eden might be re-visited (John 1:13). The seed must be replanted and allowed to germinate so that righteous fruits might be seen and harvested.

By this divine action, a new breed of mankind is generated and placed alongside the old breed. "Let them grow together until the harvest" Jesus said in His parable of the wheat and tares (Matthew 13:24-30). The children of the new Adam (Jesus), those that are re-generated, must live side by side with the children of the old Adam and Eve (or children of Satan because they are still under his spell), those who are not re-born by the Spirit, until the angels are sent to separate them.

In addition, we read in Romans 12:2 "do not be conformed to this world, but be transformed by the renewing of your mind, that you may prove what the will of God is, that which is good and acceptable and perfect". This is an essential pedigree in the restoration plan, which enables man's mind to do the divine purpose and will. A mind that is conformed to the standard and practices of this present world, actively manipulated by evil, as well as Satan, its father, does not participated in the divine plan. It still belongs to the first Adamic race. When it is transformed in the knowledge and likeness of its Creator, it focuses on heavenly things and spiritual matters; and it also learns to declare with the new Adam (Jesus). "My kingdom is not of this world" (John 18:36), symbolising that he belongs to a different world that is yet to be manifested.

Besides, Jesus said in John 17:4 "I have given them thy word, and the world has hated them, because they are not of the world even as I am not of the world" to establish this distinction. In another place it is written, "Do not love the world, or the things in the world, if anyone loves the world, the love of the Father is not in him" (1 John 2:15). Paul wrote to the Philippians' brethren insisting that the mind of Christ must be manifested through them. "Have this mind (attitude) in yourselves, which was also in Christ Jesus" (Philippians 2:5) he wrote. This is the essence of our salvation. It is therefore paramount that the old mind must come into the captivity of the Holy Spirit voluntarily, so that the new mind in Christ may be revealed in us to please God, our Father.

This new generation of people must set their minds on things in heaven where God dwells, not on earthly things, since they are now citizens of heaven. According to Paul's letter to the Philippians "Our citizenship is in heaven, from which also we eagerly wait for a Saviour, the Lord Jesus Christ" (Philippians 3:20). And the citizenship rights reads "you have come to mount Zion and to the city of the living God, the heavenly Jerusalem, and to myriads of angels, to the general assembly and church of the first-born who are enrolled in heaven, and to God, the Judge of all, and to the spirits of righteous men made perfect, and to Jesus, the mediator of a new covenant, and to the sprinkled blood, which speaks better than the blood of Abel" (Hebrews 12:22-24).

Hence the mission is completed. A new race is born, the mind of Christ is restored into man again, and a new city is founded on their behalf. Now these must "learn what is pleasing to God and not participate in the unfruitful deeds of darkness", which is of the old mind. Glory be to God.

Chapter Five

The Mind of Prayer

"And it came to pass, that as he was praying in a certain place, when he cease, one of His disciples said unto Him 'Lord, teach us to pray as John also taught His disciples" (Luke 11:2)

In the last chapter we read about God's determination and willingness to forgive man and restore him into fellowship with Himself. Hence, we have here the disciples' direct appeal to the Master, to acquire the knowledge of how to spend such beautiful time with the Father in prayer fellowship. They have seen the master spend most of His time in deep fellowship with the Father and admired His spirit.

We are not familiar with the prayer life of these lovely disciples prior to this time, or what it was like throughout their training period. But their willingness to improve and their teachable spirit to learn from the Master are conveyed in their request.

Unfortunately, there is no record of the prayer John the Baptist taught his disciples; nevertheless, it is obvious, according to their request, that John did certainly teach his disciples what to say, when they entered into praying fellowship with God. However, it seems that John's instruction was inadequate when compared to the way Jesus prayed, since we know that some of these disciples previously belonged to John.

It is also uncertain if the request was collective or personal since the name of the person that made the request was not given. We can only assume that the thought for the request reflects a group discussion among the disciples. They all are kin to learn this new method of praying. We must also bear it in mind that these disciples are Jews, and Jewish children learn to pray as early as possible.

I was privileged enough to attend a synagogue service during my visit to Italy and was amazed the way worship was conducted. I noticed that a boy, about 12 years old, was encouraged to actively participate in the reading of God's word and the worship.

I'm sure this must have been the case in Jerusalem and Galilee during the time of Jesus. The children participated in adult worship, read and memorized God's word, and prayed at both home and the synagogue. Therefore, the request for a new teaching on prayer, especially when it is different from the ones they knew from youth, and probably different to what John understood about praying, was expected. Who would want to miss such an opportunity? Not me. A time-out was needed, as well as a prayer session that all will profit from. It was a private study or instruction time that was timely requested.

The Master did not have to call a prayer-session because He knew prayer was a private relationship with God the Father that can only be maintained and enjoyed by the willing mind. It was almost an impossible task for the human natural mind to comprehend the importance of praying and appreciate it. Only the mind of Christ and the Spirit of the living God can motivate the newly regenerated man to achieve and attain this level of prayer.

Nevertheless, there was the need to learn how to communicate with God since all of mankind has failed and fallen short of the glory of God that allows such a relationship in worship. Hence, there is a need to learn how to resume communication with God, just as Adam did in the garden.

The Master, on the other hand, did not hesitate to grant their request. Through His teaching, the mind of the Master was revealed, as if to say this is the main thing I think about during My prayer time. 'When you pray, say, "Father, Thy kingdom come"' was the Master's opening speech. This is God's priority for sending Jesus into the world as well as to die for their sins. The establishment of His kingdom on earth will be made possible as earthly people demonstrate their willingness to accept His rule. If there were no earthly people to accept His rule and practice His will, His kingdom will not be established, and if the kingdom is not established on earth, the earth is doomed for destruction, and its inhabitants will be removed.

Earthly people must accept His rule and authority in order to save face and eminent destruction. What good is it to accommodate rebellious and evil people, who had the opportunity to accept His rule but bluntly refused? Unless there are remnants that accepted His rule and authority, there won't be an earth left to inhabit. Thus, the first duty in prayer is to pray that earthly people accept God's kingdom.

We have laid out in previous chapters the extent that God is willing to go in order to restore earthly people and save them from the coming disaster. All of God's effort will be useless and wasted if at the end of the day mankind turned deaf ears to the call for reconciliation and restoration. 'Thy kingdom come' must be the first cry for mercies from the disciples and eventually all of mankind. It must be the basis for the preaching of the gospel by earthly people, since that was the foundation teaching of Jesus throughout His ministry. The heart of the Father is to regain His kingdom rule on earth from the hands of the devil and the evil spirits (or rebellious angels who lost their place in the presence of God) who cunningly took it away from earthly people. As disciples of the kingdom, this must also be our focus and mission to fellow dwellers, pleading and persuading them to respond to the goodness of God in Christ Jesus.

In one of his teachings, Jesus states that "the kingdom of God is not coming with signs to be observed; nor will they say, 'look, here it is!' or 'there it is!' for behold, the kingdom of God is in your midst" (Luke 17:20,21). This was to emphasis the proximity of the kingdom. 'It is in your midst' or 'it is within you' as indicated by other translations.

If the translation 'it is in your midst' is considered, then the kingdom will point directly to Jesus as the embodiment of the kingdom. But, if on the other hand, the second translation is taken, that 'the kingdom of God is within you', the emphasis is mankind, symbolizing that there is something of the kingdom of God in man. Man has the source of the kingdom of God deeply rooted within him so that he can tap into in order to respond to the rescue package. Evidently, the presence of the rule of God is in man and if only he could fight the deception of Satan, the rule of God in him will manifest itself.

There is goodness in every earthly person, which he or she sometimes finds difficult to express because of the presence of evil. This goodness comes from the very nature of God in Adam at the beginning of creation. If we look back to the Garden of Eden we remember that the fruit that was eaten by Adam and Eve is that of good and evil; but more of evil than good since man's creation was relatively good in the image of his Creator. Jesus knew this according to His statement in Luke 6:43, which reads "For there is no good tree which produces bad fruit: nor, on the other hand, a bad tree which produces good fruit; for each tree is known by its own fruit".

Consequently, the kingdom seed is there to be revitalized and rejuvenated. Man is not far away from the Kingdom of God, Jesus told the rulers. The only obstacle is the presence of evil, which was dealt with on the cross. The bible says in 1 John 3:8 that "the Son of

God appeared for this purpose, that He might destroy the works of the devil". In another place it is written that Jesus died so that "He might render powerless him who had the power of death, that is the devil; and might deliver those who through fear of death were subject to slavery all their lives" (Hebrews 2:14,15).

In addition, it is deceptive to consider the kingdom of God as a physical entity or establishment at this time, although it shall be in the future. Essentially, it is a spiritual establishment. The spirituality of things must first be restored to obedience before the manifestation of the material establishment. God does not dwell in the house built by hand, the bible tells us in Acts 17:24,25, but in the heart of men. "You are the temple of the living God" we are told in 1 Corinthians 3:16, and this is where His kingdom is established.

Again, this brings us back to the fact that the reign of God is established in our heart and mind when we embark upon accepting and practising (doing) His will. "For it is God, Himself that works in us both to will and work for His good pleasure," says the scripture (Philippians 2:13). Therefore, it is remarkable that God, in His mercies, shall cause us to continually be willing to do and enable us to practice His will so that we may be able to please Him according to His standard; since, in the first instance, our existence was for His glory and good pleasure.

It will be a fruitless endeavour to proceed with these teachings if we disregard and despise the cry to the Father to establish His kingdom on earth. The full experience and the totality of the gospel message are rooted in this request, and must not be taken lightly. Much consideration must be given to this since it is the mind of Christ expressed in prayer. The provision and protection request for our daily needs, as found in the prayer instruction, typifies our dependence on God. Without the establishment of His kingdom in our hearts all is vanity upon vanity. The words of Jesus in Matthew 6:33 read, "but seek first His kingdom and His righteousness, and all these things shall be added to you". These words remind us what is most important to God.

Though the request for provision and protection are important needs for living, they can never be compared to the search for the kingdom of God, its establishment in our lives, and on earth at large. To us food is more important than life, but for God and Jesus, it's the opposite, since in Jesus' teaching it's life that needs food and not food that needs life (Matthew 6:25).

The apostle Paul reminded us of the importance of life and the kingdom of God, when he wrote, "food is for the stomach, and stomach is for food; but God will do away with both of them" (1 Corinthians 6:13). In another place he was disgusted with some who made their stomach (food) their god that he wrote "they are enemies of the cross of Christ, whose end is destruction, whose god is their appetite" Philippians 3:18,19.

By requesting for provision and protection in our prayer we demonstrate our acceptance of God's reign and rule in our lives. It indicates our dependence and trust in Him to meet our essential daily needs.

Prior to now, I must admit I did not understand these praying instructions. I had thought it was God's responsibility to provide for all my needs, regardless of my request for them or not. I strongly believe that I am a child of God, and He is my Father who knows whatever I need before I even open my mouth to ask Him or meditate in my heart. According to the teachings of Jesus in Matthew 6:12, that "your heavenly Father knows that you need all these things", I was rest assured that the Father is well acquainted with my essentials. Shouldn't this be the case with every child of God, I wondered? However, it is obvious in another teaching that Jesus encouraged His followers to pray without ceasing: to pray until their request is granted (Matthew 7:7-12). This seems to contradict each other.

The thought of having two conflicting statements bothered my mind until I began to see a pattern formed through the help of the Holy Spirit. First, I found in James' letter that praying has more to it than just continuously requesting for something. In James 4:1-3 we read, "What is the source of quarrels and conflicts amongst you? Is not the source your pleasures that wages war in your members? You lust and do not have; so you commit murder. And you are envious and cannot obtain; so you fight and quarrel. You do not have because you do not ask. You ask and do not receive, because you ask with wrong motives, so that you may spend it on your pleasure".

This statement doubtlessly portrays the human mind and attitude we carry with us in prayer; that of envying, fighting, wrong motive, and self-pleasure. Such a state of mind falls short of the standard of praying Jesus taught. In fact it is the opposite of every thing the kingdom of God offers. This truly demonstrates the mind and attitude of an unregenerate person as it was before the flood of Noah. Asking in prayer as taught by Jesus is not based on wrong motives and self-pleasure.

Though we may think our request is for our essentials, it is casually focused on the kingdom of God and for His pleasure. To conceive it otherwise is to deny God the glory and nullify any dependence on Him to provide and protect. According to Paul's letter to the Romans' church "the kingdom of God is not food and drink (our self pleasure)", instead it is about pleasing God "for he who in this way serves Christ is acceptable to God and approved by men" (Romans 14:17,18).

Looking again on those passages of scripture enables us to rediscover the importance of praying. We find that the acceptance of His kingly rule in our lives precedes our request for our daily needs. We cannot under estimate this reality in our prayer life that God's priority supersedes our needs. Every request must fall in line with His will, and every thing outside His will is discarded. John made this clear in his letter, which stated "and this is the confidence which we have before Him that, if we ask anything according to His will, He hears us" (1 John 5:14).

Should we now stand on the ground that our heavenly Father knows about our needs, and will provide them if we first seek His kingdom and His righteousness, or should we continue to ask whatsoever it is, hoping that He will certainly respond now that we have been redeemed by His blood? My concern is that these two positions, as highlighted, have important implications in our prayer lives, as one suggests communion and trust, and the other suggests communication and trust.

A child in communion and trust explicitly seeks to rely on the father's adequate judgement to evaluate and provide his or her essentials whenever the father deems fit, while his or her endeavour is to please the father in righteousness. An example to such a position is our children who trust us to provide what is needed for their comfort without any swindling. Of course these were the days when children were children with little or no environmental pressure from technology. Jesus Himself attested to this when He said, "let little children come to me for theirs is the kingdom of God" (Matthew 19:14). Obviously Jesus was able to relate to this and compares the absolute trusting power of a child to that of the kingdom.

On the other hand, we know that as children grow into their teens, they take matters into their own hands, sometimes indicating their preferences, due to their awareness of their environment. This is when passages like James 4:1-3 come into play in our family life, just as it does in God's family. Sometime parents fail to meet their children's demands either because they cannot afford it, or because it is not in-line with the essentials of life. This same selfish demanding attitude we deploy in our prayer life, especially if we were brought up to have our ways and demands. Subsequently, we make our request by giving our Father a lists of what we want, and demanding He provide them because He has promised to grant us whatever we ask. Some go a little further by giving God a time to deliver the goods.

Of course this also is communication and trust. But where is the childlike relationship when God is considered a manipulative business partner that has no will or discipline or direction? Reflecting on John's statement, God has a will as well as direction. He is the King of the castle and has rules that His subjects abide by; and He is not lonely in His domain that He longs for our adoption to keep His companionship.

I know a married couple that took the stand not to buy a car, although they can afford it. The lady was my superintendent at my place of work. One day I asked my superintendent why they spend so much on a taxi, both for them and their two daughters when they can afford a car. She replied 'it is cheaper to take a taxi than to own a car. All that we need is within our locality, and whenever we feel like going to the centre of London, a day's travel card does the job'. They sometimes walk to their local big store, buy food and things for the family, and take a taxi home. Their children were happy with this arrangement, and wherever they travel they had no need for a car.

Not many of us have such a mind that is not pressurised by our environment even when we cannot afford the lifestyle we crave for.

When I could not afford to drive our car because we could not afford to buy the car's insurance, it seemed strange to my wife to travel to church on Sunday on the local bus. She felt our standard had been compromised and we would lose face amongst friends and family. To be candid, our use of the car was limited to shopping at the local stores on Saturday and going to church on Sunday; every other day of the week we used the local transport. There was pressure to get the car back on the road, even though we could not afford it, since we have our reputation to protect.

Therefore, it is clear that our environment plays an important part in our lives, especially our prayer lives as children of God. Thus, I paused one day to inquire from the Holy Spirit the purpose of praying if God already knows our needs and wants. It wasn't as if I lack the understanding and knowledge most Christians have; I just felt there is much more to praying than communication and asking for things. I knew that communicating with the base at all times were essential, yet I needed direction. So I waited for some spiritual insight form the Holy Spirit.

Not long after, I began to realize that prayer has its peak, and its priority is fellowship. In fact, the essence of praying is fellowship and relationship with the Father, rather than a social call to a charity centre. It is our very existence.

This was what was lost in the Garden of Eden. It was not communication with Adam that was missing, since we know God continued to communicate with Adam after he sinned. It was the fellowship and friendly relationship that was gone. God came to fellowship with Adam, but he was no longer at the place of meeting. They both communicated, but at a distance. Therefore, it was important that Jesus should bring up the issue in the 'Lord's prayer', teaching the disciples that God is in search of a family bond. Besides, most of His other teachings are tied up in this Father-son relationship. For instance, in the teaching in Matthew 7:7-12 regarding asking, seeking, and knocking; He wrapped it up in family bond, that of a son asking for bread and fish (daily provision of essential needs) from his father, and the father meeting the son's request.

Every time Jesus prayed, the peak of His prayer is close in relationship with the Father. He never does anything outside the Father's knowledge. The family bond was there, and this gave Him access to the throne of grace. Accordingly, Hebrews 4:16 instruct us to "boldly come to the throne of grace to obtain mercies and help during our time of need". But how can we come boldly without first securing relationship with the Father? How can one be bold to request something from someone you hurt daily? Yet we do come with our tails between our legs to beg for mercy.

This only reminds us of the story of the prodigal son who remembered his father and the services his father offers to strangers, when he was desperate to survive, while his father was daily concerned of his safety and whereabouts. With all the money he had with him, he did not send his father a letter or greeting card, though people travel daily to their home-town. There was never a time he was home sick during his pleasure days. Nevertheless, the father never stopped longing to hear from him. At a glance, he rushed to welcome him.

We treat God in the same manner, only coming home to Him during our desperate moments. Though He does not complain, He does occasionally hint to us that the bonding is out as solid as He expected. Jesus took this same attitude with some of His followers who claimed they have been searching everywhere for Him. To these excited seekers He replied, "Truly, truly, I say to you, you seek Me, not because you saw signs, but because you ate of the loaves, and were filled. Do not work for food which perished, but for the food which endures to eternal life, which the Son of Man shall give to you, for on Him the Father, even God, has set His seal" (John 6:26,27).

To shamefully crown it, they all decided to leave Him, when He gave them the food that leads to eternal life, though they claimed they were searching for Him (John 6:66). There is nothing wrong with prayer that requests for provision and protection, but there are richer blessings when our prayer life is moved to the level of relationship with the Father. When was the last time you went on your knees in prayer and said to the Father 'I have nothing to request today'; or wait silently to hear your heartbeat before Him? Some Christians call it spending time with the Father to listen to His problems and how He felt about it.

These are moments when God enters into fellowship with His child; and they are indeed best times. Jesus told His disciples to watch with Him in prayer during His hour of pain and agony. To read that the Master had inner emotions as He confronts the cross, and shared it with His disciples, makes things clearer to us that God sometimes wants us to listen to Him.

One last thing to consider is the statement in Romans 8:26a which reads "for we do not know how to pray as we should, but the Spirit Himself intercedes for us with groaning too deep for words". If we do not know how to pray, as we should, according to this passage, though we sometimes scream and pray in our pain, there must be something missing in our prayers. Perhaps they are presented with the wrong motive and contain selfish ambitions. Nevertheless, these are petitions presented to God from our sincere emotional heart and there should be a response from God, who has the right to grant or reject or amend or suspend them until the right time. This is where the Holy Spirit comes in to modify and enhance our request along the will of God.

We tend to forget this aspect when we quote this passage in support of our supplications. The reason is that some of us do not know where the passage is in scripture and make an attempt to read it; while some have read it but did not make further effort to read the next verse. Owing to this, we lack understanding of the operation of the Holy Spirit in prayer.

I have seen some Christians grunt in prayer as to indicate the groaning of the Spirit. However, I doubt if this was Paul's idea or if we truly know how the Spirit groans to our heavenly Father in prayer on our behalf. Thus, to understand this ministry of the Holy Spirit, we need to read the next verse, which states "and He (God) who searches the hearts knows what the mind of the Spirit is, because He (Spirit) intercedes for the saints according to the will of God" (verse 27). I have emphasized on the words 'the will of God' because it is written in a different style from the other word, not because I chose to. For me, and many others, if not all, the stress on 'the will of God' tells a deep and fundamental point when we pray.

With this view in mind comes two main important points worth noting. The first is that God searches our heart when we offer our petitions to Him if they are packaged according to His will or packaged in wrong motives and selfish ambition. If they are acceptable, the request has passed the test for consideration. Second, where these are shortcomings, He searches the mind of the Holy Spirit living in us to find out exactly what our request was; and the Holy Spirit repackages them in line with the will of God for our lives. So we have John declare in his epistle "if we ask (make our request) according to His will, He answers us" (1 John 5:14).

God, our heavenly Father, does not just give us things because we requested them, but grants requests on the ground that our request is part of His will for us. Therefore, we need the mind of the Holy Spirit, which also is the mind of Christ in prayer, to enable us discern the will of God when we pray.

I grew up, as a Christian, with the simple concepts of prayer that God answers all prayers with these three words: 'yes', 'no', and 'not yet (pending)'. But as time went by, another concept entered my mind that states 'prayer changes things'. Some believers went a step further to state that 'prayer changes all things'. As a teacher of the word of God I was concerned about these new concepts, not because I do not believe that prayer changes things, but because if by praying we can change things, where does the will of God fit in, with regards to universal orderliness and God's pre-planned activities? There is a section in the bible that states that all things are possible with God and those that have faith, and there is another section that states we must ask according to His will (1 John 5:14).

There must definitely be a balance somehow and somewhere. Consequently, I kept meditating and chewing up both facts in my heart, waiting for enlightenment from the Spirit. At first, I attempted to balance both thoughts with the phrase 'prayer can only change things that God had pre-plan or earmark to be changed'. This is good, I thought to myself, because I found a neutral ground, still upholding the thought that only God's will prevails in this matter of prayers.

But some days later God, in His mercies, gave me some understanding through my wife. We had a discussion about answers to prayers. She had the belief that prayer changes things; I felt this was the best time to

71

drop my neutral ground into the discussion. So I shared it with her. But she was adamant to change her stance that 'prayer changes things'. I tried to convince her that changes come only if our request is according to the will of God.

I cited scriptures in support of my understanding, making particular reference to Jesus' agonizing prayer to the Father, to take the cup away, but He concluded that the Father's will must be done. She replied with the words 'if Jesus had persisted in His request to have the cup taken away from Him the Father would have done it, and looked for another way to rescue us. It then means that Jesus was disobedient to the Father's will and wanted His own. Prayer essentially changes things, even things that are not according to God's will, but there are always repercussions for our disobedience'.

With her statement I was able to clearly see how prayer does change things, whether according to the will of God or not, because we persistently desire to have what we want. A typical scriptural support to this is found in the book of the Kings of Israel. The corporate was King Hezekiah in 2 kings 20. Hezekiah was ill to the point of death and also heard a confirmation from God that he was going to die. Instead of accepting the will of God for his life, he prayed and wept bitterly, telling God how righteously he had served Him all his life. Within seconds, God changed His mind and answered his request to live. So God healed him and gave him more years.

Consequently, the extended years led to a curse on his reign, which was fulfilled in the days of his son who became king after him. How did this happen? It was during these extended years of his reign that he opened the door to the enemy by showing the Babylonians the treasures of Israel. God was not pleased with him for this action. So He sent the prophet Isaiah to him with the statement "hear the words of the Lord, behold the days are coming when all that is in your house, and all that your fathers have laid in store to this day shall be carried to Babylon, nothing shall be left" (2 kings 20:16-17). What a price to pay for refusing God's will for his life. He should have accepted the verdict of death God placed on him. Instead, he brought a curse on his family instead of blessings. Unfortunately it was his successor that paid the price.

Prayer truly changes things, but we must seriously consider that very situation we desperately want to change, in case that is God's will for us at that time. For He knew the present situation is for our benefit, and will lead to a better future. Since we do not know what is best for us, or able to see what lies ahead in the future, we must endeavour not to cause God to turn aside His will for our lives. Difficult times may come our way, but God, who has designed them to be, knows how to make away in due time.

Like our Master, the Lord Jesus Christ, we must cultivate the attitude of yielding completely to God's will by saying "My Father, if this cup will not pass away unless I drink it, Thy will be done" (Matthew 26:42).

Paul did the same thing when he prayed three times for an illness to be removed or healed. Instead he received the message "my grace is sufficient for you" (2 Corinthians 12:9). I'm sure if he had persisted in prayer, refusing to receive those words for encouragement, God would have healed him. But he knew what it was to do and accept God's will for one's life. We must definitely pray according to His will; this is the mind of Christ. Though we so much desire our requests to be answered, our true and sincere confession must be 'have it Your own way Lord, have it Your way'.

There are many Christians who have learned how to pray according to the will of God because they know the mind of Christ regarding the situation they are presenting to the Father. For such, God will not take the time to search their hearts and consult with the Holy Spirit (so to say) before their request is granted because they have the mind of Christ. Their thinking faculty is intoning with that of the Holy Spirit; and if there were any additions or improvements, the Holy Spirit will waste no time to alter them. May God grant the mind of Christ in us to grow speedily into maturity. Amen.

Chapter Six

The Mind's Attitude to life – Living

"They drink their fill of the abundance of Thy house; and Thou dost give them to drink of the river of Thy delights. For with Thee is the fountain of life" Psalms 36:8,9

*I*n the previous chapters we examined how God successfully restored man's mind to the mind of Christ. Since He was not going to pronounce judgement and impose punishment on all mankind for their sin, He embarked on the plan of enlightening them and taking their punishment Himself. In John 1:9,29 we read "there was the true light which, coming into the world, enlightens every man. The next day John saw Jesus coming to him and said 'behold the Lamb of God who takes away the sin of the world'".

God has finished carrying out His plan, the question now is will mankind accept this plan of mercies, and cooperate with God? Remember, His plan was not to be imposed on man, but must be made freely available. Man must be free to make a choice to either accept the plan and sign the dotted lines in obedience to Him or reject it, and continue with his rebellion; and face future consequences, which is God's wrath and punishment.

Merely accepting the plan and receiving the mind of Christ is not all that is required, man must be determined to live out his life the way Christ did during His earthly days. Philippians 2:5 says "have this attitude in yourself which was also in Christ Jesus", and carried on to speak about the humility of Jesus. Previously it has said "only conduct yourselves in a manner worthy of the gospel of Christ" (Philippians 1:27). Therefore, the mind of Christ includes both humility and an attitude that is pleasing to God. God Himself testified to this when He publicly declared, "this is my beloved Son in whom I am well pleased" (Matthew 3:17).

Looking intensively into chapter two of Philippians, and the first four verses, we have a catalogue of useful index used to present the mind of Christ. Here it speaks about 'encouragement in Christ', 'consolation of love', 'fellowship of the Spirit', 'affection and compassion', as the bottom rock of our faith in Christ Jesus. These were embodied in Christ's mind and teachings. It was not that of selfishness, or empty conceit that overrates self and undervalues others, but that of humility of the mind that promotes the welfare and interest of others. It was not only the humility of suffering and pain of verses 5-11 that is to be emulated, but in addition those of the first four verses that depicts the lifestyle of Jesus on earth: that of encouraging others, love, affection, compassion, and fellowship with the Holy Spirit. All these teachings are found in Jesus' sermon on the mountain. One of the major conclusions of the sermon "just as you want people to treat you, treat them in the same way" (Luke 6:31) stands out as the golden rule in the kingdom of God. Paul agrees with this principle when he instructed Christian "do not merely look out for your own personal interest but also for the interest of others" (Philippians 2:4). The same thing is written in 1 Corinthians 10:24 "let no one seek his own good, but that of his neighbour".

This is contrary to the world we all live in today where the favourite statement is 'looking after number one'. It is a dramatic change from the lifestyle we know. The scriptures clearly state that in the last days "men (mankind) will be lovers of self, lovers of money, boastful, arrogant, brutal, haters of good, reckless, treacherous, conceited, and lovers of pleasure rather than lovers of God" (2 Timothy 3:1-4). These and many more are the pictures of today's lifestyle. Everything is selfish ambition with less consideration for others.

Nevertheless, God has given us this challenge to live a Christ-like lifestyle in our environment in order to attain His plan and purpose for mankind. We are to let our light shine before all mankind so that they may glorify our Heavenly Father (Matthew 5:16). We are to be the heavenly ambassador on planet earth since He has granted us the citizenship of heaven, proving to all that we are strangers and aliens of this planet.

A popular Christian songwriter (Jim Reeves) declared his stand for the heavenly kingdom when he sang 'this world is not my home, I'm just passing through, if heaven is not my home Oh Lord what should I do. I can't feel at home in this world any more'. This should, and is the confession, of all who seek the heavenly calling. This world is a long distance from home; therefore, we must not dare forget to continuously live the heavenly lifestyle. Neither must we partake with unbelievers by letting immorality, or any impurity, or greed even, be mentioned among us (Ephesians 5:3). Colossians 3:1-2 clearly points out this fact, demanding our complete focus on our citizenship in order to propel us into good ambassadorship. It states "if then you have been raised up with Christ keep seeking the things above where Christ is seated at the right hand of God. Set your mind on the things above, not on the things that are on earth".

If Jesus had set His mind on earthly things and glory, particularly when Satan gifted him on a platter, He would have failed completely, and mankind would have been without a Saviour. Thank God He focused on heavenly things 'and the thing on earth became strangely deemed'. Nothing in heavenly places or on planet earth was going to deter or distract Him from the heavenly vision and commission. This was why He came into the world; this was why He was born, and failure was not an option. How easily we get distracted with the pleasures of this present world, and desire to participate in it, thereby forgetting who we are and our homeland – the heavenly city. According to the bible, we have come into the household of God (Hebrews 12:22), that holy city that was the longing of all saints.

Certainly 'the last days' have reckless living, yet we must keep living by that godly standard to which we were called and granted the mind of Christ. Therefore, it is vivid that the mind of Christ was given so that we may be able to overcome the pressures of this present world. It is a serious business, a matter not to be taken lightly. God expects nothing less than the lifestyle of Christ from us. To be honest, we did not have the fullness of the mind of Christ when we became born again, but a potential seed of the mind of Christ to be nurtured, groomed, and grow into maturity. This is why we have 'ups and downs' in our Christian walk with God. Some days we are Christ-like, and some other times we fall short of the standard.

But the potential to reach that full maturity is there. For this reason God ordained pastors and teachers to enable us to "attain to the unity of the faith, and of the knowledge of the Son of God, to a mature man, to the measure of the stature which belong to the fullness of Christ" (Ephesians 4:11-13).

I have met and spoken to many Christians who honestly admitted that the early days of their Christian life were better than where they are at present. The reason for such an assessment was that they found themselves losing interest in godly matters compared to the early days when they were on fire for God and the kingdom of heaven: longing for spiritual milk and growth, like a baby who eats frequently and regularly. This Christ-like lifestyle, which was prominent, begins to dwindle down, as we become older and confront more hardships that test our faith. But this should not be the case. The hardship and testing were meant to progress our development in Christ and improve the Christ-like lifestyle. In fact they are meant to fortify our standing in the Lord according to James.

We all have a similar story just like this, where our Christian walk with God had become a struggle. The reason for this is found in the letter of Paul to the Galatians, stating, "The flesh sets its desire against the Spirit and the Spirit against the flesh; for these are in opposition (conflict) to one another, so that you may not do the things that you please (want)" (Galatians 5:17). Truly, we have the old master (the mind of the flesh) in conflict with the new master (the mind of the Spirit of Christ) trying to dominate our lives; but we make the decision as to who should win the conflict. When we yield dominance to the flesh, we struggle so much, given that the blood of Christ redeem us, and fulfils the desires of the flesh was not part of the deal. But when the Spirit of Christ is in control, we become masters over the Flesh. Just as it is written, "walk (live) by the Spirit, and you will not gratify the desires of the sinful nature" (Galatians 5:16). In another place it is written "for all who are being led by the Spirit of God, these are the sons (children) of God" (Romans 8:14).

As we grow older in the faith, God's expectation of the Christ-like life increases: yet, this is the very time we fail because we are tricked by the flesh to taking God's mercies for granted. Instead of walking in the Spirit like we did when we first became Christians or born-again, we fall into the trap of complacency and droopiness that has been introduced by the enemy.

Our devotion begins to slide and our services take a tumble. Slowly the old life begins to creep in, leading us to gratify the desires of our old sinful nature, thereby resulting to lukewarm (neither cold nor hot). Though we still feel as if nothing has happened that changed our direction, we match out to battle, like Samson in Judges16:20, to fight the enemy. Jesus said to the Laodicean's church "because you are lukewarm, and neither hot nor cold, I will spit you out of my mouth" (Revelation 3:17) indicating the seriousness of our walk with Jesus.

People that live the godly life do not measure their relationship with God in material blessings or good health, though God promises to bless His children. Instead, they learn through suffering and obedience to be content in whatever situation they found themselves. They declare with Paul "I have learnt to be content in whatever circumstances I am. I know how to get along with humble means, and I also know how to live in prosperity; in any and every circumstance I have learned the secret of being filled and going hungry, both of having abundance and suffering need" (Philippians 4:11,12).

This is the view and the teachings of Jesus when He taught us not to worry about what we shall eat or wear like the unbelievers do, but rather we should seek "the kingdom of God and its righteousness" (Matthew 6:33).

A preacher said his daily request to God is to 'have roof over my head and clothes on my back, and food in my stomach'. This indeed corresponds to the teachings of Jesus. The writer of the Proverbs 30:8,9 attested to this simplicity.

If you assume this is a new kingdom principle that was not practised by Old Testament saints, you are wrong. Though it was God's wish to bless them richly, they never asked or demanded it. They continued to disregard the pleasure of this world and focused on that which was to come. Holding firmly to their faith they declared, "they are aliens and strangers in this world" (Hebrews 11:13). Accordingly, we have supplications, like the one written by a godly man in Proverbs 30:8-9, which reads "keep deception and lies far from me, give me neither poverty nor riches, feed me with the food that is my portion, lest I be full and deny Thee and say 'who is the Lord?' or lest I be in want and steal, and profane the name of my God" for our learning, and to enable us to walk righteously (upright) with God.

We constantly refer to those who receive God's blessings, asking God to bless us alike, but it is clear in scriptures that not one of these saints requested blessings, or failed to acknowledge God in their misfortune, or desired it so much that they were not prepared to let go of it in order to be at peace with their neighbours. An example is Isaac who gave up his well in order to maintain peace (Genesis 26:18-22). It is also written of Moses that he chose "to endure ill-treatment with the people of God, than to enjoy the passing pleasures of sin (as the son of Pharaoh' daughter)" Hebrews 11:24-26.

In fact the words of the Prophet Habakkuk sums it up as he joyfully declared "though the fig tree should not blossom, and there be no fruit on the vines; though the yield of the olive should fail, and the fields produce no food; though the flock should be cut off from the fold, and there be no cattle in the stalls; yet I will exult in the Lord, I will rejoice in the God of my salvation" (Habakkuk 3:17-18). Such statements truly show these saints were not after God for material wealth, but for righteousness. This is unlike the church in Laodicea that had all the wealth, but was not rich towards God because the fruits of righteousness were not there amongst them; the god of this world (Satan) had blindfolded them. They have used wealth as the measuring rod for God's approval for righteous living. May God, in His mercies, deliver us from the spirit of spiritual deception. Amen.

God planted His seed in us at the beginning of the new creature, to see it grow from seed to the tree. He intends bringing forth fruits of righteousness (maturity). Therefore, we must not abandon the young tree to gratify the old nature. The scripture states "His divine power has given us everything we need for life and godliness... in order that by it we may become partakers of the divine nature, having escaped the corruption that is in the world by lust" (2 Peter 1:3-4).

This indicates the heart of God and His plan for our spiritual development. This is the divine purpose for us, and we must stop drifting backwards into the world and all it has to offer. His kingdom and lifestyle must not be ignored as we walk and live according to His Spirit within us, not embarking on our own mission of improvising righteousness (making our own rule and living life in our standard).

The Psalmist wrote that the godly man is "like a tree firmly planted by the stream of waters, yielding its fruits in its season, while its leaves does not wither (even in the winter months), and in whatever he or she does he or she prospers" (Psalm 1:3). This refers to the steadfastness of a person who is in step with the Almighty, and walking in the strength of His righteousness as provided by the Holy Spirit.

Therefore, by living and walking in the Spirit the seed of God in us is nurtured and grows into maturity; empowered and sustained by the Spirit. He alone is capable of nurturing our minds to grow to the measure of the stature that belongs to the fullness of Christ. Hence, the warnings "not to walk like the worldly people walk, in the futility (vanity) of their mind, practising every kind of impurity with greediness" (Ephesians 4:17-19); instead, we are to be "renewed in the spirit of our mind, and put on the new self, who in the likeness of God has been created in righteousness and holiness of the truth" (Ephesians 4:20-24).

A much better picture of this 'kingdom living (lifestyle)' is illustrated in the parable Jesus told about a farmer who went about his business sowing seeds (Matthew 13:1-9, 18-23). The importance of this story is that it indicates the level of each Christian in the kingdom. Some will hear the message but waste no time to lose it because the enemy is there to devalue its worth;

so they cast it aside hoping to take matters into their own hands. Some others will temporarily welcome the teachings, but fail to nurture the seed so that it may have roots in them and produce the life God intended. For this group, hardship in life, insults for being a Christian, and not being serious with the kingdom lifestyle was sufficient reason for falling aside. But the third group had a different dilemma. They had too much thought about the life they left behind, its lifestyle and pleasures, that it drowned and drained the divine life from them. Owing to this, they were unable to walk in the spirit with the Spirit in them, and were succumbed to the deceitfulness of worldly riches and pleasure, or were they able to win the battle of the desires of the flesh (Galatians 5:16). For this reason, their plant had no chance of surviving the competition for the good soil, hence the unfruitfulness. Their holy plant was choked to death. An example for us is found in the person of Demas who loved this present world and fell off the grace of God. Writing to Timothy regarding Demas, Paul wrote, "for Demas, having loved this present world, has deserted me" 2 Timothy 4:10.

However, the fourth group did everything right according to the will and purpose of God; they walked and lived in the spirit and with the Spirit, and possessed the mind of Christ in its fullness that enabled them to produce the fruit of righteousness and godliness. Their seed was nurtured and grew to maturity, enjoying abundant life as promised by Jesus. "I came that they might have life, and have it abundantly" Jesus affirms in

John 10:10, so that His followers may understand that He is the source of lasting prosperity. This group produced fruits of righteousness and holiness that delighted God's heart.

Chapter Seven

The Mind of Giving

"Give and it will be given to you; good measure, pressed down, shaken together, running over, they will pour into your lap: for by your standard of measure it will be measured to you in return" Luke 6:38.

Every Sunday I listen to the pastor of my local church plead with the congregation to give their offering to God. He has just finished preaching the word and praying for those in need of ministering as well as those who are deeply touched by his message. Unfortunately, he must do his best to convince us, born again Christians, to part with our money for the progress of God's work on earth. Why should he have to do this every Sunday I pondered in my heart? My one thought was that he shouldn't have to do all this pleading and persuasion if God is truly our Father, and we have just received encouragement from Him. We certainly have this responsibility to Him and His ministers to provide for the work He has called us to do.

As Christians we are aware of the basic way He has chosen to meet such a responsibility, but do sometimes allow our senses to override our spiritual responsibility because we try to convince ourselves that He understands our situations and needs. Of course He understands that we are shunning our responsibilities and disobeying His ordinance. He also understands that we have failed to honour Him with our substances, thereby forcing Him to withhold His blessings on both our family and us. "Honour the Lord from your wealth, and from the first of all your produce; so your barns will be filled with plenty, and your vats will overflow with new wine" declare the writer of Proverbs 3:9,10.

I hope we also understand that our prayers are not answered because He is angry and seeks revenge, but that He seems to be occupied with other serious matters that require His attention or one of His faithful servants is in greater need; thus, He has to prioritize His time. Though He said 'before you call I will answer', He only offers this service to those who have first honoured Him in obedience; not only in giving our money, but also in accordance with the teachings of Christ.

In my view, and according to scriptures, we should determine in our hearts what to give before we come to church, and in some cases, we may be prompted by the Holy Spirit to give more during fellowship. We may not have the extra, but we can assure the Holy Spirit we will do it next time we come together to fellowship. All is in the mind; and the state of our mind and its attitude towards the things of God, determines our relationship with God and how much we love Him. The ones that mind the things of the kingdom of God save into the heavenly bank; knowing that whatever is there will be needed when they get to heaven. Those that mind earthly fame invest into this present world hoping to harvest nothing when they get to heaven, if they actually make it there.

If we truly love God, our love must definitively reach down into our pockets and purses. This is what Christ would have done if He were with us in the flesh, because He dearly loves the Father. In fact, it is worth saying that giving is an attitude of God that causes Him to release His blessings to all mankind, for His hand is forever open and ready to give. This is the mind of Christ and that of the kingdom of God which God expects all His children to posses. Failure to have this mind causes us to struggle in our expression of love to God through our giving. Because we have at the back of our minds that it is our 'hard earned money', we hold back and ask ourselves why we should part with it.

I have used the term 'hard earned money' to indicate that such mind is worldly, not of Christ, and to shame us for accommodating such thought. In simple language, we are saying that anyone who desires our money must have to earn it. Even God must have to prove He deserves to earn it. We forget the saying that states "all things come from Him and they are all His.

There is a story in the bible about a man that possessed such mind, and found it difficult to part with his food. His name is Nabal, which means 'worthless'. In the story, 1 Samuel 25, David had requested a share in the fortunes of Nabal since he had a bounty harvest. In reply, Nabal sent David's men away empty handed, shamed, and with the message 'who is David and who is the son Jesse? Shall I then take my bread and my water and my shears, and give it to men whose origin I do not know (Verse 10,11)?'

When David got this humiliating message he was extremely furious and decided to kill every thing that has breath in Nabal's household. When Nabal's wife, Abigail, heard what her husband had done, she immediately acted positively to rescue the situation. Thank God for such wives who are always there to mend their husband's foolishness and rescue the day. Her wise action and persuasive words were sufficient to stop David from carrying out his plan. But this did not stop God from carrying out an appropriate judgement, sentencing Nabal to death. Who then was rewarded with his 'hard earned money'? Abigail, of course; she is the one who had willingly taken the step to share with unknown faces.

We have many Nabals in our society and few Abigails. People who find it hard to part with their possessions because they have worked hard for them, and have become vain in their thinking; they are tight-fits, merciless, and do not have the mind of God and Christ. These spell out Nabal's lifestyle. It is there in the bible that there is someone that withholds, yet runs into poverty and another that scatters, yet lacks nothing (Proverbs 11:24).

I am sure none of us will receive anything from God if He takes into consideration whether we earned it or not. Rather, He willingly gives us everything through Jesus our Lord. The bible says "He has freely blessed us with heavenly blessing" (Ephesians 1:3). And in another place it reads "He who did not spare His own Son, but delivered Him up for us all, how will He not also with Him freely give us all things?"

Since this is the attitude God takes towards us we are indebted to reciprocate in a similar fashion. The scriptures affirm "God loves a cheerful giver" in2 Corinthian 9:7, and that "it is more blessed to give than to receive" (Acts 20:35). None of us mind receiving gifts and blessings from God and man, but the honour and joy belong to the giver, especially when the gift is from a cheerful heart and not by compulsion.

I have listened to messages where people are encouraged to give because God has promised to bless them abundantly in return. Such messages are supported with statements that some did not receive because they were not in expectancy. This is not necessary the case. Sometimes our packages arrive in different shapes and colours we did not expect. Therefore, not appreciated because it wasn't the parcel we wanted.

One thing is certain from scriptures, God does bless His people whether they expect it or not, because He hates to be indebted to anyone. Accordingly Romans 11:35 emphasises that "no one gives to Him and does not receive in return", regardless of the giver's state of mind, because He is bound by His words. On the other hand, there are some that give, either to God or fellow humans, just because they love giving and blessing others, and posses the joy of being there for someone, without any expectants of payback from God. They are likened to the man in Proverbs 11:24, which reads, "There is one who scatters yet increases all the more".

They love God so much that they refused to keep any record of their giving. They are sure, beyond any doubt, that He is indebted to no man, and will keep His promises. The giving and receiving principle is both clear and guaranteed.

The statement of Jesus "give and it will be given to you" (Luke 6:38) is enough assurance that God will re-pay without any drop of sweat from us. It seems we are so conscious of our childhood experience with our parent's unfulfilled promises, which prompt us to say to them 'dad, mum, you promised'. Thus, forgetting who God our heavenly Father is, we treat Him like our earthly parents. God never commits Himself to a project and abandons it when the going gets tough. He never gives His words and turns away from them when its time to fulfil it; nor does He owe any man or withhold due payments. Instead, He gives beyond our dreams and expectations, though it may not be in the manner we expect.

His blessings are not always measured in pound sterling or dollars, but manifested in numerous ways beyond our imagination. Good health is an example of His blessings, as is satisfaction and joy in the spirit. So the songwriter said 'count your blessings and name them one by one' to support the manner in which God subscribes to payback. The assurance of payback is there, written in concrete, and established on the rock (Jesus). It is as sure as our pay slips. The only time we complain is when there are no pay slips to confirm payment into our account. Even then the accountant reassures us that payment has been made into our banks, and pay slips will follow shortly.

Godly men in scripture, such as Abraham, used this complaint system to remind God of His promises, seeking reassurance. Genesis15: 2,3 reads "And Abram said, 'O Lord God, what will Thou give me, since I am childless, and the heir of my house is Eliezer of Damascus? Since Thou hast given no offspring to me, one born in my house is my heir'". First, Abraham states his case that his trusted slave will inherit everything he had worked for because God has not given him a son as promised. In response, God reassured him that he would surely have a son by stating "This man will not be your heir; but one shall come forth from your own body, he shall be your heir" Genesis 15:4. Abraham once again believed God, and God recorded this act as Abraham's righteousness. All Abraham had to do was believe God regarding His promises and be obedient, while God worked out how to keep His promised words.

Expectancy is good when we know what to expect; but when we do not know what package to expect or the content of our package we acknowledge the delivered package as the best for that period. Disappointment comes when the package does not meet our expectation because we expect likes for likes from God. But God determines what is best for us for that season because of

His love for us. He may multiply it in another season; but the assurance of multiple blessings is guaranteed. He understands what we need or want but also knows the stages of delivering, as well as the first package to deliver. Hence we have to trust and believe Him like father Abraham did.

When the statement of Paul to the Corinthians is considered: "God is able to make all grace abound to you, that always having all sufficiency in everything, you may have an abundance for every good deed" (2 Corinthians 9:8), we begin to understand that the blessings from God are not 'like for like', but abundant grace in everything. Let us finally take heart in the words of our Lord Jesus regarding giving, as found in Matthew 6:1-4, knowing that our Father who sees our secret giving and knows the secrets of our hearts, will repay us with the full package. This is the mind of Christ to envy and possess.

An interesting comment was made about Jesus' attitude by John the Apostle in John 13:28,29, during the last super that is worth mentioning, since it draws our attention to his practice. This reads "now no one of those reclining at the table knew for what purpose He had said this to him (Judas), for some were supposing because Judas had the money box, that Jesus was saying to him 'buy the things we have need of for the feast'; or else, that he should give something to the poor".

The simplicity of this comment indicates that the disciples are aware of the daily practices of Jesus to give arms to the poor in the community when they are spotted. Hence His teaching that we should give without expecting a pay back since this has a great reward. His instruction is "Give to everyone who asks of you, and whoever takes away what is yours, do not demand it back; so good, and lend, expecting nothing in return; and your reward will be great and you will be sons of the Most High" Luke 6:30. Keep up the mind of Christ in you and you will be flabbergasted with God's abundant blessings.

Chapter Eight

The Mind of Appreciation

'In everything give thanks' (1Thessalonians 5:18)

You will agree that there is plenty to be thankful for in our lives and the lives of our families and friends, but does this plenty include the words 'all things' as started in 1 Thessalonians 5:18? I remember a great man of God relating to us his experience of this verse of scripture. He told us how he had boldly preached on this text many times in his ministry to the churches encouraging Christians to thank God in whatever situation they are in, but never thought he would be tested.

One day in his travelling, the opportunity came for him to practice what he had been preaching when he discovered the airline he took has misplaced his luggage. You remember that catch phrase 'Physician (Doctor) heal your self' became the order of that day. We also know that some Doctors don't like taking medications just like some patients. The preacher was like that when it was his turn to take his own medication. He was very angry and offended, using strong language, and burning hot and cold as his jacket became unbearable to put on.

When he finally began to calm down, the Holy Spirit spoke gently into his heart and asked him about his preaching 'give thanks in all things'. At this point he realised he had not practised what he preached to others, and was ashamed of himself. Though no one there knew him as a preacher of the gospel or ever heard his teachings on giving thanks in all things, the Holy Spirit reminded him.

The majority of us, Christians, can easily relate to this experience since we've all sometime and somewhere, lost our calmness in Christ because of the situation confronting us. I recently had the story of the Christian who wrote the lovely song 'it is well with my soul' that the inspiration to write the song came when he was told his son had died in a boat accident. What a blessed and encouraging song it has been over the years to many Christians undergoing difficult times and praising God in their situation. The challenges of life become deemed as the soul focuses on its Saviour. These are the times when giving thanks in all things is applicable.

If I were asked what my favourite film is, I would simply reply - 'Pollyanna'. The film Pollyanna was about a little girl aged twelve or there about, who arrived in a town to stay with her aunt because both of her parents died in a car accident. Her spirit and attitude to life changed the attitude of the people who lived there. She had been schooled by her father, who was a church minister, on the topic of 'giving thanks in all things'. Her catch phrase was 'lets find something to be thankful for' as she approached adults going through hard times. Her father always told them that there is always something in every tough situation in life to be thankful for. Not long after, her catch phrase spread widely into the community as everyone both young and old, searched for something in their situation to express appreciation to God.

Of course, these situations might be painful and upsetting, yet the scripture encourages us to be grateful or find something in that very situation that could lead to praise, applying Pollyanna's catch phrase. This has been the practice of godly men and women in the bible. Take, for an example, the situation of David in 2 Samuel 12: 1-23, when he heard the news of his beloved son's death. To the shock of his officers, he was not badly upset by the news. Instead, he had a bath and ended his fasting. His statement to his officers was "while the child was still alive, I fasted and wept; for I said 'who knows the Lord may be gracious to me that the child may live.' But now he has died why should I fast? Can I bring him back again? I shall go to him, but he will not return to me" 2 Samuel 12:22,23.

Job, in his terrible situations, did the same thing and Abraham would have gladly offered his only son if God had allowed him. Paul also spoke about the joy in the hearts of the Hebrew Christians who suffered the loss of their possessions due to persecution. He wrote to them stating "For you showed sympathy to the prisoners, and accepted joyfully the seizure of your property, knowing that you have for yourselves a better possession and an abiding one" Hebrews 10:34.

Besides all these referrers is the most important fact of it all: giving thanks in all things is linked with the will of God for our lives. I recently discovered this essential point when I listened to a minister's wife teaching, making reference to this passage in Thessalonians. When she finished reading this first part of the verse she stopped and continued with her teachings, but I read a step further to discover that the most important aspect of giving thanks in all things is that God wills us to do so. The second part of the verse reads "for this is God's will for you in Christ Jesus" (1 Thessalonians 5:18b).

It was at this point that 'the penny dropped' and my eyes lightened up. In simplest language, this is what God wants me to do as a Christian. Another way to express it is to say 'this attitude and action, giving thanks in everything, pleases God because it is what He wants from me as a Christian'. Our duty as Christians is to fulfil our Father's desire since it is clearly stated that this is the wish of God for all His children in Christ Jesus. This probably is the reason we have statements such as "Rejoice always, and I will say again Rejoice" (Philippians 4:4) or "the joy of the Lord is your strength" (Nehemiah 8:10) written in bible.

God wants His children to know and have the assurance that not a single hair on their head falls off without His knowledge and approval. According to Jesus "The very hairs of your head are all numbered" Mathews 10:30. With such assurance the Christian's joy is boundless. May He continue to strengthen us in the inner man, to joyfully carry out His wishes in every tough situations of life. Remember, tough situations are meant to toughen our character, and produce grace that embarrasses Satan. Not that he, Satan, will slacken off the pressure for this reason, but our resilience will certainly allow God to be proud of us, and the angels applaud our confidence. Thus we laugh at the face of disaster like godly men of old, such as Daniel and the three Hebrews in Babylon's fire. "Bring it on" we say to Satan in confidence; and to God, our Father, we celebrate like the apostle, giving Him praise for counting us worthy to partake in the suffering of Christ. It is our calling in Christ Jesus to give thanks in all things, for it is the will of our heavenly Father for us. Amen.